THE BEATLES

By Michael Burgan

WORLD ALMANAC® LIBRARY

Please visit our web site at: www.garethstevens.com
For a free color catalog describing World Almanac® Library's
list of high-quality books and multimedia programs,
call 1-800-848-2928 or fax your request to (414) 332-3567.

Library of Congress Cataloging-in-Publication Data

Burgan, Michael.
    The Beatles / by Michael Burgan.
       p. cm. — (Trailblazers of the modern world)
    Includes bibliographical references, discography, and index.
    Summary: The story of the highly celebrated and influential English rock group and their music.
    ISBN 0-8368-5068-8 (lib. bdg.)
    ISBN 0-8368-5228-1 (softcover)
    1. Beatles—Juvenile literature. 2. Rock musicians—England—Biography—Juvenile literature.
    [1. Beatles. 2. Musicians. 3. Rock music.] I. Title. II. Series.
    ML3930.B4B87   2002
    782.42166'092'2—dc21
    [B]   2001045629

Updated and reprinted in 2005
This North American edition first published in 2002 by
World Almanac® Library
330 West Olive Street, Suite 100
Milwaukee, WI 53212 USA

This U.S. edition © 2002 by World Almanac® Library.

An Editorial Directions book
Editor: Lucia Raatma
Designer and page production: Ox and Company
Photo researcher: Dawn Friedman
Indexer: Tim Griffin
World Almanac® Library art direction: Tammy West
World Almanac® Library production: Susan Ashley and Jessica L. Morris

Photo credits: Corbis/Bettmann, cover; Corbis/Hulton-Deutsch Collection, 4; Corbis/Bettmann, 5; Corbis/Norman Parkinson Limited/Fiona Cowan, 6–7; AP/Wide World Photos/Museum of Television and Radio, 8; Hulton Archive, 9 top, 9 bottom; Corbis/Hulton-Deutsch Collection, 10; Hulton Archive, 11; Corbis/Bettmann, 12; Hulton Archive, 13, 14; AP/Wide World Photos, 15; Hulton Archive, 16; Corbis/Bettmann, 17; Corbis/Hulton-Deutsch Collection, 18; Hulton Archive, 20 top; Corbis/Hulton-Deutsch Collection, 20 bottom, 21, 22–23, 23 right; AP/Wide World Photos, 25, 26; Corbis, 27 top; AP/Wide World Photos, 27 bottom; Hulton Archive, 28; AP/Wide World Photos, 29; Corbis/Bettmann, 30; AP/Wide World Photos, 31 top, 31 bottom; Hulton Archive, 34 left; AP/Wide World Photos, 34 right, 35, 36, 37; Hulton Archive, 38 top; AP/Wide World Photos, 38 bottom; Hulton Archive/Express Newspapers, 39; AP/Wide World Photos, 40 top, 40 bottom; Hulton Archive, 42 top; AP/Wide World Photos, 42 bottom, 43.

Printed in the United States of America

3 4 5 6 7 8 9 10 09 08 07 06

TABLE of CONTENTS

Words that appear in the glossary are printed in **boldface**
type the first time they occur in the text.

CHAPTER 1

ROCK 'N' ROLL HEROES

Rock 'n' roll was born in the 1950s, but during the 1960s, it became the favorite music of teenagers around the world. More than any other single group, the Beatles shaped the direction of rock music during that decade. Even today, collections of their songs sell millions of CDs.

The roots of the Beatles go back to Liverpool, England—birthplace of John Lennon, Paul McCartney, George Harrison, and Ringo Starr. This lineup of the Beatles first recorded in 1962, and by 1964, **Beatlemania** swept the world. The group was influenced by many earlier rock stars, such as Buddy Holly, Chuck

The Beatles had their beginning in their hometown of Liverpool, England.

Berry, and Elvis Presley. The band members also knew other kinds of music besides rock 'n' roll, such as jazz, **blues**, and the old tunes played in English music halls. The Beatles took all the musical styles they knew and loved and combined them to make rock music that was fast, loud, and fun.

WORLDWIDE FAME

The Beatles' energy quickly grabbed the attention of young people everywhere. Kids could dance to the beat and sing along to the memorable melodies. The Beatles' music also stirred many teenagers to grab a guitar, learn a few **chords**, and try to make their own music. After the Beatles, many rock 'n' roll artists felt they had to write their own music and play their own instruments to be taken seriously. Before them, many popular singers could succeed by recording other people's music, as long as they had a pleasant voice and a pretty face. Beatlemania also unleashed a wave of music from England—the **British Invasion**—that brought new energy to the American music scene.

In 1966, the Beatles changed direction. They stopped touring so they could concentrate on their recordings. They also showed more interest in so-called serious music, experimenting with new recording techniques and borrowing musical ideas from India. Their song lyrics changed, too. McCartney and Lennon, the group's major songwriters, stopped writing about teenage love and instead told stories about people and places. Some of the songs still dealt with love, but they addressed the topic in a more sophisticated way. As the Beatles grew up, so did their music. With each new album, fans, critics, and other musicians eagerly waited to see what new direction the Beatles had taken.

Beatlemania excited fans all over the world.

SPLITTING UP AND MOVING ON

Being part of a group for more than a decade was not always easy. The band members wanted to try musical projects on their own. Over time, McCartney and Lennon virtually stopped writing as a team, though both their names were always listed on the records. They and the other band members sometimes argued over their songs and the record company they had formed. By 1969, John, Paul, George, and Ringo knew the Beatles were over, and the band officially broke up the next year.

The Fab Four in 1964 (left to right): George Harrison, Paul McCartney, Ringo Starr, and John Lennon

All four members of the Beatles continued recording music individually. Still, fans always hoped the band would get together to play one more concert or record one last song. Any thought of a Beatles reunion died on December 8, 1980, when John Lennon was shot and killed outside his New York apartment. Fans of both Lennon and the Beatles mourned his death.

After that, the other three band members occasionally recorded together, until George Harrison's death in 2001. The Beatles will always be remembered as trailblazers of popular music.

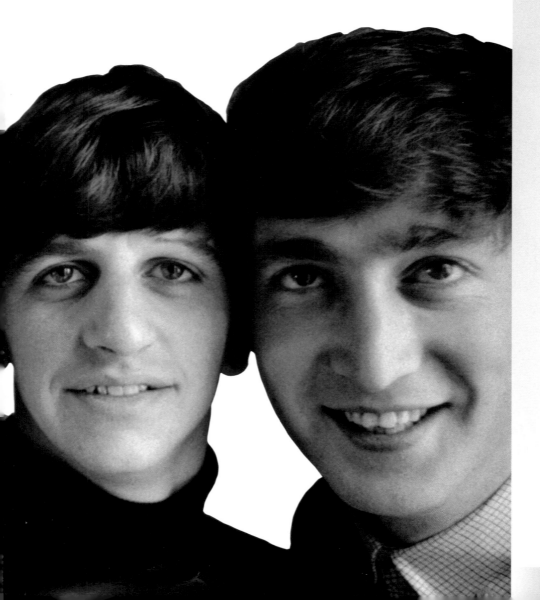

CHAPTER 2

THREE LADS FROM LIVERPOOL

The music of Elvis Presley had a big impact on John Lennon.

In 1956, a teenager in Liverpool heard music that changed his life. John Lennon enjoyed country music and a type of British folk music called **skiffle**. Then he heard Elvis Presley sing "Heartbreak Hotel." "Nothing really affected me until I heard Elvis," John later said. "If there hadn't been Elvis, there would not have been the Beatles."

Presley, from Mississippi, was the first huge star of rock 'n' roll. He blended country music with several forms of music developed by African Americans, such as **rhythm and blues**, jazz, and **gospel**. All these types of music were common in the South. Presley and other performers mixed these styles to bring rock 'n' roll to the mainstream of popular American music in the 1950s. White singers, such as Presley, Carl Perkins, and Buddy Holly, and black artists, such as Chuck Berry and Little Richard, influenced many young Liverpool musicians. The English teens embraced the energy and strong beat of rock music.

John was born in Liverpool on October 9, 1940. His musical career began when he was a boy, playing the harmonica and the accordion. As a teenager, he formed a skiffle band named the Quarry Men. By then John was playing guitar, though he didn't take any lessons and had to borrow an instrument. Finally, he convinced the aunt who raised him to buy him a guitar. She told her nephew, "The guitar's all right for a hobby, John, but you'll never make a living at it."

Chuck Berry performed a style of music that influenced the Beatles and many others.

PAUL AND GEORGE COME ON BOARD

Teenage John Lennon as a member of the Quarry Men

The Quarry Men performed in public for the first time in June 1957, when they tried out for a local talent show—and lost. At the group's third performance, in July, one of the band members introduced John to a friend named Paul McCartney. Soon, Paul was a Quarry Man, too.

Paul was born in Liverpool on June 18, 1942. As a child, Paul heard music all the time, both live and on the radio. His father had once played trumpet in a jazz band, and the McCartneys owned a piano. Paul learned to play both of those instruments, though he never learned to read or write music. As a teen, he traded his trumpet for a guitar. Since he was left-handed, he learned to play it upside down. Paul wrote "I Lost My Little Girl," his first song, when he was fourteen.

Paul first performed with the Quarry Men in October 1957. When his first solo came, the new guitarist panicked and could not play the notes. The band realized they needed a better guitarist, and Paul suggested his friend George Harrison. Born on February 25, 1943, George had met Paul on the school bus. Like Paul's family, the Harrisons enjoyed music and often played

The King of Skiffle

As much as John, George, and Paul liked American blues and rock, they became musicians because of skiffle. This type of music was popular in Great Britain during the 1950s. Using a guitar and perhaps a washboard and a banjo, skiffle bands played simple blues and folk songs. The most popular skiffle musician of the era was Lonnie Donegan (left). In 1956 he recorded an old American folk tune called "Rock Island Line" that became a hit in England. In 1958, his song "Does Your Chewing Gum Lose Its Flavor (on the Bedpost Overnight)" became a hit in England and was popular in the United States a few years later. "When we were kids in Liverpool," Paul said, "the man who really started the craze for guitar was Lonnie Donegan." The Quarry Men played several songs that Donegan had recorded, including "Midnight Special" and "Worried Man Blues." At age seventy, Donegan was still performing in Great Britain.

records and the radio. George bought a guitar and took lessons from a family friend.

When he auditioned for the Quarry Men, George played an instrumental rock tune called "Raunchy." "He got out his guitar," Paul later said, "and sure enough, he could play it, and everyone agreed, 'you're in.'" By now the band was playing less skiffle and more rock 'n' roll. John, Paul, and George shared a passion for this new style of music coming from America. They became the core of the band as other musicians came and left. Paul and John also wrote songs together, and some of these early tunes were later recorded by the Beatles.

The Quarry Men did not have many live shows during 1958 and 1959, playing mostly at private parties. At one point in 1959, the group became a trio, with George, Paul, and John playing without a drummer. The group performed at a talent contest in Manchester, England—their first show outside of Liverpool. Paul and George played guitar as John sang. Once again, the group did not win the contest. The future did not look especially bright for the Quarry Men, but their fortunes soon changed.

Selling the Quarry Men

In October 1957, a friend of the Quarry Men tried to get the band a job at a local club. He wrote a letter to the club owner:

The "Quarry Men" have done very well in a short period of time. They have appeared in the Carol Levis show [their first talent contest], also many clubs in Liverpool including the "Cavern," and I feel sure that this group is well up to standard. It's a five piece group and they play Skiffle, Rock 'n' Roll and Country Western. I hope to hear from you soon.

George, John, and Paul in the years before Ringo

CHAPTER 3

ON TO GERMANY

Stu Sutcliffe played bass for the Beatles but later left the band.

The Quarry Men started 1960 as a quartet, with Stu Sutcliffe joining the band on bass. John was attending art school, and Sutcliffe was his roommate. A talented artist, Sutcliffe enjoyed books and films, but he could hardly play his instrument. Still, John wanted him in the band.

Soon after, the Quarry Men changed their name to the Beatles. The group played several times in the spring of 1960, using a part-time drummer. In August, the band had the chance to play in Hamburg, Germany, so it recruited a full-time drummer named Pete Best. His mother owned a club where the Quarry Men had often played. Best is sometimes called "the fifth Beatle," though Sutcliffe has also been given that name. While they were part of the band during its early years, neither Best nor Sutcliffe ever shared in the Beatles' real success.

Why "Beatles"?

Beatles experts—and the band members themselves—have disagreed over how the band got its name. Some people credit Stu Sutcliffe alone, while Paul said both Sutcliffe and John coined the name. John claimed the credit for himself. Supposedly, he and Sutcliffe were influenced by Buddy Holly, who called his band the Crickets. John and/or Sutcliffe decided to change the name "Beetles" to Beatles to suggest the importance of the beat in their music. At one point, the name was spelled Beatals, and the band also used Silver Beetles and Silver Beatles before settling on its final name.

The German job looked like a great opportunity. Each band member was promised 15 pounds (about $40) a week, which was more than some of their fathers earned, but life in Hamburg was not so glamorous. The city, like Liverpool, is a major seaport. The Beatles played at clubs in a poor section of Hamburg filled with criminals and run-down bars. The band members lived in an old movie theater, and their room was next to the toilets. The Beatles played for eight hours a night, and the club owners wanted them to put on a show, not just play music. The group responded by jumping around on stage as they played and telling jokes between songs. Overall, the band members accepted—even enjoyed— the harsh conditions and their experience in Germany. John later said, "I grew up in Hamburg, not Liverpool."

Hamburg is also where the Beatles met Ringo Starr. His real name was Richard Starkey, but he used "Ringo" as a nickname because he often wore several rings, and he later shortened his last name. Born in Liverpool on July 7, 1940, Ringo had come to Germany with a group

Ringo Starr (far right) in 1962, as a member of Rory Storm and the Hurricanes

called Rory Storm and the Hurricanes. He had learned to play drums as a teenager, while spending a year in a Liverpool hospital recovering from a lung disease. Ringo met John, Paul, and George in Hamburg when the Beatles and Ringo's group played at the same club. In October 1960, Ringo and another member of his band made a record with the Beatles, but it was never released.

By then, the Beatles had many German fans. The band played rock 'n' roll songs with tremendous energy, and the members grew more confident in their talents. An argument with a club owner, however, ended their stay in Hamburg, and by December all the Beatles except Stu Sutcliffe were back in Liverpool. Stu remained in Germany until February, and he played with the group only a few more times after that. Stu Sutcliffe died in 1962 from a brain injury suffered in a bad fall.

THE BEATLES TAKE SHAPE

With Sutcliffe gone, Paul began playing bass. The band spent the early part of 1961 playing clubs in Liverpool, and they soon became one of the city's hottest acts. The group also went back to Hamburg for three months. During that time, the Beatles recorded several songs with Tony Sheridan, an English singer the band had met on its first trip to Germany. The Beatles also adopted a new look, wearing black leather and cowboy boots and letting their hair grow long.

After returning to Liverpool, the Beatles continued to play local clubs, where they were often advertised as "the Fabulous Beatles." (Later, the group was sometimes known as the "Fab Four.") In the fall of 1961, a local radio station played "My Bonnie," one of the songs the Beatles had recorded with Sheridan. A few teenagers requested the song at a record store managed by Brian Epstein. A curious Epstein then attended a Beatles show at the Cavern Club. Although not a rock 'n' roll fan, Epstein knew something about music. In addition to running the store, Epstein wrote a music column for a local paper. He saw that the band had charm and talent. By January 1962, he was their manager, even though he had no experience running a band. Epstein, however, had a good business sense, and he promised the Beatles better jobs at a higher salary.

Brian Epstein was enthralled by the Beatles and went on to become their manager.

Brian Meets the Beatles

In a 1964 radio interview on the BBC, Brian Epstein described his reaction to seeing the Beatles for the first time.

They were rather scruffily dressed . . . black leather jacket and jeans, long hair of course. And they had a rather untidy stage presentation . . . not terribly aware, and not caring very much, what they looked like, I think they cared more even then for what they sounded like. I immediately liked what I heard. They were fresh and they were honest, and they had a presence and . . . star quality. Whatever that is, they had it, or I sensed that they had it.

opposite: Outside the Cavern Club, shown here in 1966, a nightspot in Liverpool where the Beatles sometimes performed

The Beatles in 1961; Pete Best (second from left) was the band's drummer before being replaced by Ringo Starr.

Epstein tried to make the Beatles more professional. He told them to arrive on time for their concerts and stop clowning around on stage. He also replaced their leather jackets with gray suits and thin black ties. Despite this outward change, the Beatles still played rock 'n' roll. They also began playing their own songs, not just their versions of other musicians' records. At the time, none of the groups in Liverpool played their own music. Paul later said, "We were making ourselves into a group that was different."

Epstein worked hard to get the band a recording contract. The band taped fifteen songs during an audition for Decca Records. The company was not impressed and rejected the band. An angry Epstein told Decca officials, "You must be out of your minds . . . I am completely confident that one day they will be bigger than Elvis Presley!"

After Epstein tried several other companies, the Beatles signed a contract in June 1962 with EMI Records. Earlier, the band had its first radio appearance on the British Broadcasting Company (BBC), Great Britain's national radio channel. The Beatles' first TV appearance followed later in the year. The band also made the last change in its lineup. Pete Best missed a few performances because of illness, and Ringo replaced him. "Every time Ringo sat in," George later said, "it seemed like 'this is it.' Eventually we realized we should get Ringo in the band full time. " Best had never truly fit in with the others, lacking their wit and playful personalities. Ringo was a much better match—and a better drummer—so he joined the Beatles for good in August 1962.

In October, the new version of the Beatles released their first record. On one side was "Love Me Do." The **flip side** had "P.S. I Love You." John and Paul wrote both songs. "Love Me Do" reached number seventeen on one London newspaper's **record chart**, and the Beatles were named Liverpool's most popular band of 1962. The group finished the year playing one last concert in Hamburg, then prepared for even more success.

The Beatles sporting their clean-cut look

CHAPTER 4

THE BIRTH OF BEATLEMANIA

Early in 1963, the Beatles released their second record, "Please Please Me." The band had wanted to record it as the flip side to "Love Me Do," but the group's **producer**, George Martin, disagreed. When the Beatles went to record their second single, Martin wanted to do a song written by someone else, but the Beatles pleaded with him to use one of their own songs. Martin finally suggested that the band record "Please Please Me," but at a faster tempo than John had written it. Everyone agreed the new version was better. Martin told the band, "You've got your first number one." He was right—by February "Please Please Me" was number one on the record chart published by *New Musical Express*, a leading British music magazine.

Producer George Martin joined the Beatles in celebrating the quarter-million sales mark for "Please Please Me" in 1962.

The Man in the Studio

Pete Best, Stu Sutcliffe, and Brian Epstein have each at various times been called the "fifth Beatle." George Martin, however, was the person most important to the Beatles' music who often shared that nickname. Martin started working as a producer for EMI in 1950, recording comedians as well as classical and jazz musicians. He produced the Beatles throughout their career. At the first recording sessions, Martin listened as Paul and George played their songs on **acoustic** guitars, then he made suggestions and had the final say on which songs the band recorded. Even after the Beatles gained more independence on their recordings, they relied on Martin's advice regarding which instruments to use or how a song should sound. Still, the Beatles also trusted their own instincts. Paul recalled that Martin sometimes told the group they couldn't use certain chords, and they would ignore him, saying, "We like it man; it's bluesy."

In the meantime, the Beatles hit the road, traveling through England and Scotland to play concerts. "A lot of madness went on in the van," Ringo later said, "but it got us together." The four musicians would need that friendship, as their lives soon became chaotic.

After earning their first number-one hit, the Beatles recorded their first album, also called *Please Please Me*. They worked almost nonstop for twelve hours and finished it in one day. The album was released in March, and it eventually became the best-selling record in Great Britain, staying at number one for thirty weeks. The album that knocked it out of the top spot was another Beatles product, *With the Beatles*.

The Beatles' music had energy and a sense of fun. In person, the band members were witty and charming. Some teenaged girls thought they were cute, and most fans enjoyed the band's driving beat and sweet melodies. Some music critics analyzed the Beatles' music and found sophisticated structures—musical ideals the group had not deliberately tried to use. The Beatles just

In 1963, the Beatles' fan club in London was inundated with mail for the Fab Four.

John Lennon and Cynthia Powell in 1965

wrote music that made them—and their fans—feel good. Still, no one could completely explain the group's sudden popularity and the adoration they stirred in their fans.

Throughout 1963, the band played more concerts in larger halls and appeared frequently on radio and TV. For a while the Beatles had their own weekly radio show on the BBC. By the end of the year, the Beatles had a fan club and a monthly magazine that tracked their every move. Beatle fans searched for any bit of information about the band and acted on what they learned. At one show, the members of the audience showered the band with jelly beans, after George had reported that he liked that sweet treat.

The fans also learned about the personal lives of the Beatles. In 1962, John had married Cynthia Powell, and the couple had a son, Julian, in April 1963. Brian Epstein had tried to keep the marriage a secret, so female fans would not lose interest in John or the band. He did not have to worry—swooning girls still screamed John's name.

The interest in the Beatles even included their relatives. In mid-1963, George treated his parents to a vacation in Jamaica. As they rested on the beach, a stranger approached the Harrisons. "He was a reporter," Mrs. Harrison later said. "I woke [Mr. Harrison] up. I said there's a reporter taking all your snores down."

Lennon in 1967 with his son Julian, who went on to be a musician as well

Beatlemania in Action

A London paper published this report of an October 1963 Beatles show.

Nearly 2,000 teenage girls, screaming "We Want the Beatles," battled through a panting police cordon outside the London Palladium last night.

The battle reached its climax minutes after the curtain came down at the close of ITV's Sunday Night at the Palladium.

Since mid-morning, Liverpool's Beatles group . . . had been prisoners in the Palladium while the teenagers surged outside.

Extra police stood at the gangways while more sealed off the stage door.

But when the Beatles, with their bobbed haircuts, finished their 12-minute set, the trouble really started.

Screaming girls launched themselves against the police—sending helmets flying and constables reeling.

Police vans sealed off the front of the theatre so that the Beatles could be smuggled out.

By October 1963, London newspapers began publishing articles on the great success of the Beatles and the screaming, adoring fans they attracted. One reporter coined the term *Beatlemania* to describe the reaction to the group. The interest in the band spread to the highest levels of British society. In November, the Beatles played a concert for the Queen Mother of England and other members of the royal family. Before the last song, John said, "I'd like to ask your help. Would the people in the cheaper seats clap your hands? And the rest of you, if you'll just rattle your jewelry." John's joke was aimed at the rich and powerful people in the audience, but they did not mind. Afterward, the Queen Mother said the Beatles were "so fresh and vital. I simply adore them."

The hit records continued through the end of 1963, and so did the hordes of fans that followed the group. The Beatles made money with all their success—the band sold more than $13 million worth of records just in Great Britain, but that success came at a high price. The band required police protection in public to keep away the crowds. Fans stole

opposite: Beatles' fans, shown here straining against a line of London police officers outside Buckingham Palace, could often be an unruly bunch as they waited to see the famous group.

At a performance for the British royal family

clothes and instruments from their dressing rooms. On stage, the fans' shrieks drowned out the music, and the band members could not hear themselves sing. Ringo said, "I remember we were in a cage at [one show] because it got so crazy. It was like being in a zoo, on stage! . . . It was the first time I felt that if they got near us, we would be ripped apart."

While the Beatles enjoyed tremendous success in Great Britain, they were still almost unknown in the United States. The band's record company, EMI, had a U.S. branch called Capitol Records. George Martin recalled that as the Beatles recorded their hit songs, he tried to convince Capitol to sell the records in the United States. "And each time," Martin said, "the head of Capitol would turn it down: 'Sorry we know our market better than you do, and we don't think they're very good.'"

Several small U.S. record companies, including Vee Jay and Swan, did release some Beatles songs, but they did not sell well. (Some of these songs, such as "Please Please Me" and "From Me to You," were released again after Beatlemania reached the United States and became hits.) Most Americans heard of the Beatles for the first time at the end of 1963, when the major U.S. television networks sent camera crews to report on Beatlemania in Great Britain. Soon, Americans would see and hear the Beatles for themselves.

The Beatles and the Press

John offered an explanation of why he disliked many newspapers and reporters during the early days of Beatlemania.

We were funny at press conferences because it was all a joke. They'd ask joke questions so you'd give joke answers. . . . If there were any good questions, about our music, we took them seriously. Our image was only a teeny part of us. It was created by the press and by us. It had to be wrong because you can't put over how you really are. Newspapers always get things wrong. Even when bits were true it was always old. New images would catch on just as were leaving them.

CONQUERING AMERICA

In November 1963, Brian Epstein arranged for the Beatles to appear on *The Ed Sullivan Show*, a successful Sunday-night **variety show**. Although the Beatles were not popular yet in North America, Sullivan thought his viewers might be interested in seeing the four "mop tops" (a reference to the Beatles' long hair—or what seemed long in 1963).

The Beatles' world changed dramatically before they made their first live appearance on U.S. television. On December 26, Capitol released its first Beatles single, "I Want to Hold Your Hand." It quickly became a huge hit, selling a million copies in just a few weeks. On just one day in New York City, fans bought 10,000 copies every hour. While the band toured France, their song hit number one on the U.S. record charts. "We couldn't believe it," Ringo later said. "We all just started acting like people from Texas, hollering and shouting 'Ya-hoo!'" Sales of older Beatles songs also began to increase in the United States.

The Beatles waving to fans from their window in New York's Plaza Hotel before their first appearance on *The Ed Sullivan Show* in February 1964

Even though their records were now selling well, the Beatles were not sure how they would do in "the States." One English reporter said the band asked him, "America's got everything . . . so why should they want us?"

The Beatles had also created some enemies. Some critics and parents thought both their long hair and their music were offensive. In the song "She Loves You," the band often repeats the words "yeah, yeah, yeah." To some Americans, this slang proved the Beatles were uneducated and not appropriate for young people. Yet once the Beatles reached the States, the band's critics lost out to millions of fans.

With Ed Sullivan before performing on his popular variety show

ED SULLIVAN AND BEYOND

On February 7, 1964, the band landed in New York. Waiting for the Beatles was the largest assortment of TV cameras, photographers, and journalists the band had ever seen, along with 10,000 fans. At a press conference, the reporters asked questions, and the Beatles replied with jokes. One reporter asked what they thought of Beethoven, the nineteenth-century composer, and Ringo replied, "I love him. Especially his poems."

Two days later, the Beatles made their first appearance on *The Ed Sullivan Show*. About 700 people filled the studio, out of the 50,000 who had applied for tickets. Meanwhile an estimated 73 million Americans watched at home—television's largest audience ever at that time. For the rest of the year, the Beatles were one of the biggest news stories in North America.

Many people have tried to explain the Beatles' appeal to Americans in 1964. As in Great Britain, the

band won over young girls with their looks and charm. Other fans enjoyed the music because they could dance to it. The Beatles liked to have a good time, and that quality came through in their music. Just a few months before the Beatles came to New York, the United States had been shocked by the killing of President John F. Kennedy. The Beatles helped cheer people up. Paul later said, "I think that . . . the spirit of the Beatles seemed to suggest something youthful and fun."

The band also gave a boost to rock 'n' roll. Even though rock 'n' roll was first played in the United States, many of its early stars were no longer recording. Buddy Holly and Ritchie Valens had died in a plane crash in 1959. Little Richard stopped performing to become a preacher. Chuck Berry served time in jail. Elvis Presley was still around, but his sound had softened. He rarely recorded songs with the raw, bluesy feel of "Heartbreak Hotel."

The Beatles appeared on *The Ed Sullivan Show* on February 9, 1964.

Fans greeting the Beatles at the Los Angeles International Airport in August 1964

The music scene did have some rising stars in 1964. The Beach Boys rode a wave of popularity with their "surf music." This California band sang about cars and surfing, and like the Beatles, they showed a sense of fun. Several bands out of Detroit, such as the Temptations, the Miracles, and the Supremes, played a style of rock that was influenced by rhythm and blues and was later called the "Motown sound," a reference to the name of the record company that recorded these groups. The Beatles, however, recaptured the original energy of rock 'n' roll. They played fast and loud and reintroduced the power of electric guitars to pop music. They also added their own touches, such as playing chords rarely used in rock music, and Paul and John often sang together, creating tight vocal harmonies.

The Beatles also had good timing. The United States was at the end of its **baby boom** period, when families had more children than they'd had decades before. Babies born after World War II and during the early fifties were now teens, and they had money to spend on records and new fads. As Beatlemania came to the States, the teens wanted to be part of this new musical revolution.

The Beatles played two concerts in the United States in February 1964, then returned in the summer. They also played concerts in several other countries. Somehow the band still found time to write and record new songs, appear on radio shows, and make a movie.

Other popular singers had made movies before. Most of these films were meant to cash in on the singers' popularity and give them a chance to promote a new song. The Beatles' *A Hard Day's Night* also had these goals, but film experts agreed that the movie was better than the typical rock film. Using humor and music, the film showed what it was like being the Beatles and trying to survive Beatlemania. The band members seemed

A Hard Day's Night appeared in movie theaters all over the world.

relaxed as actors, especially Ringo, and he later made several other movies without the Beatles.

By the end of 1964, the Beatles had six number-one hits in the United States. During one week in March, the top five songs on the charts were by the Beatles—a feat no musical act has ever repeated. American teens spent an estimated $50 million that year on Beatles records and merchandise. Beatlemania ruled America. It also opened the door for other British rock bands to come to the United States, beginning the so-called British Invasion. These bands also helped bring rock 'n' roll music back to its roots.

CONTINUED SUCCESS— AND CHANGES

The Beatles started 1965 as the most successful rock 'n' roll band ever. They made another film, *Help!*, and released an album of the same name. A U.S. company also created a weekly cartoon with the Beatles as characters. They toured the United States again, and Beatlemania was still in full

Party Dangers

During the Beatles' first trip to America, they went to a party hosted by Great Britain's ambassador to the United States. A newspaper article from the *Ottawa* (Canada) *Citizen* describes some of the event.

One woman in a long dress produced a pair of scissors and snipped some hair off the head of one of the Beatles. She went off, squealing in a half-demented way, "I've got his hair . . . I've got his hair. . . ."

Lady Ormsby-Gore, who had watched the mauling of her four guests, later took one aside and apologized for the scene. "You couldn't have had much fun down there," she said.

The one who had his head shorn, Ringo Starr, merely fingered the spot where the hacking had been and said: "What a riot."

Shooting *Help!* in the Swiss Alps

swing. When the band landed at Houston's airport, fans rushed out onto the runway. "Within minutes," George wrote in his autobiography, "with us all inside, the crowds had climbed on the wings and they were knocking on the outside of the windows, and then falling off the wings."

The Beatles concert at New York's Shea Stadium drew more than 55,000 fans—a record at that time for a rock concert. By this time, however, the band no longer enjoyed touring. The group wanted to concentrate on exploring new musical styles in the studio.

During its first U.S. tour, the band had met Bob Dylan. He was considered one of the best young songwriters in America, singing about political ideas and everyday events in a poetic way. Listening to Dylan's songs, John and Paul realized they should try to write more meaningful lyrics. After hearing Dylan, John said, he used his lyrics to "try to express what I felt about myself." Dylan, in turn, was impressed by the Beatles. "They were doing things nobody was doing," he said. "I knew they were pointing the direction where music had to go."

Bob Dylan's style and lyrics influenced the Beatles' music as the group matured.

Lennon and McCartney still wrote some songs together, but more and more each wrote separately. George also began to write songs for the group to record. The Beatles also started to use instruments usually found in orchestras, not rock bands. Paul's song "Yesterday" was the first Beatles song to feature a violin and cello. This slow song about a man who has lost his girlfriend became another number-one hit. Over the years, many singers have recorded it, and "Yesterday" is now the most-recorded song in history.

In 1965, George Harrison introduced the band to music from India. He played an Indian instrument, the **sitar**, on several songs. Around 1967 George said, "We are involved not only in pop music but all music, and there are many things to be investigated."

The Beatles continued to try new approaches to their music as they recorded their next album, *Rubber Soul*. On "The Word," producer George Martin played a **harmonium**—perhaps the first time this keyboard with **reeds** was used on a rock record. "Norwegian Wood" showed John trying to be more poetic with his lyrics, as he wrote about a man struggling to connect with a woman. For "Think for Yourself," Paul used a device called a fuzz box to give his bass a distorted sound. All these little things made *Rubber Soul* sound unlike any other Beatles album—or any other popular record of the time. The music was still rock, but it sounded more creative. The band members were always thinking of ways to be different. Even the album cover was unusual for the time. The band's name was not mentioned, and the picture of the four Beatles showed their heads stretched out of shape.

On August 23, 1966, the Beatles performed at New York's Shea Stadium to a record-breaking crowd.

George Harrison with a sitar, an Indian musical instrument featured in some of the Beatles' songs

Writing for Help

In a 1980 interview, John talked about how he felt at the time the Beatles made the movie and the album *Help!*

The whole Beatle thing was just beyond comprehension. . . . When Help! came out, I was actually crying out for help. Most people think it's just a fast rock 'n' roll song . . . later I knew I really was crying out for help. . . . You see the movie: He—I—is very fat, very insecure, and he's completely lost himself, And I am singing about when I was so much younger and all the rest, looking back at how easy it was.

Rubber Soul, released in December 1965, reached number one on the charts in both Great Britain and the United States. George later said, "I think that it was the best one we made. We certainly knew we were making a good album." To others, however, the Beatles' most important music was still to come.

GOOD TIMES AND BAD

By 1966, the Beatles were no longer simple lads from Liverpool. They had traveled the globe, met famous people, and earned more money than they ever thought possible. The group also learned how much attention the world paid to what they did and said. A comment that John made about the Beatles being more popular than Jesus Christ stirred controversy in the United States. A few radio stations stopped playing Beatles songs, and some people urged fans to burn the group's records. John finally apologized for his remark in August, as the Beatles began their final U.S. tour. Brian Epstein also issued a statement, assuring Americans that "what [John] said, and meant, was that he was astonished that in the last fifty years the Church in England, and therefore Christ, had suffered a decline in interest. He did not mean to boast about the Beatles's fame."

Just a few days before, the group had released its most complex album to date. *Revolver* showed how the group was continuing to grow. The Beatles had learned more about music and electronics and wanted to apply this knowledge to their sound. The group used strings and horns, and George once again played sitar. The band also played "backwards" on "Tomorrow Never Knows" and several other songs. The band members recorded voices and instruments, then played the tape backwards and recorded that sound. Like *Rubber Soul, Revolver* showed other musicians that rock 'n' roll could be broadly defined. Not everything had to sound like old Chuck Berry or Elvis Presley tunes. Musicians could use rock as a form of art, expressing their feelings and thoughts as they experimented with new techniques for creating music. They could also borrow freely from other musical styles. The Beatles showed it was possible to try new things and still make good music that sold millions of records.

After the last U.S. tour, each of the Beatles briefly went his own way. George traveled to India to study music and religion, while Paul wrote music for the movie *The Family Way* and John acted in the film *How I Won the War*. Ringo was the only one who took a break and relaxed with his family. (He had married Maureen Cox in 1965, while George had married Pattie Boyd earlier in 1966.)

right: Ringo Starr with his wife, Maureen, and their son, Zak, in 1965

far right: George Harrison and Pattie Boyd were married in January 1966.

SGT. PEPPER

As 1967 began, Paul came up with an idea for a new album. The Beatles would pretend to be another musical group called Sgt. Pepper's Lonely Hearts Club Band. "So, when John walked up to the microphone to sing," Paul later recalled, "it wouldn't be the new John Lennon vocal, it would be whoever he was in this *new* group, his fantasy character."

Once again the Beatles tried to create a record different from any they had made before—and unlike anything else ever done in rock music. The band used more **overdubbing** than it had in the past. A few instruments were recorded at a time, then others were added later on. The group also added ringing alarm clocks and animal noises. An orchestra appears on several songs, and for one part of "A Day in the Life," Paul encouraged the musicians to play whatever they wanted at the same time. "The result was a crazy big swing storm," he said, "which we put together with all the other little ideas." Throughout the recording sessions, the band members eagerly made suggestions on what words to write or what instruments to play. Describing the Sgt. Pepper era, Ringo said, "The great thing about the band was that whoever had the best idea (it didn't matter who), that would be the one we'd use."

For the album cover, the band members dressed in old, colorful military uniforms. They also included the words to all the songs, which no rock group had ever done before. When *Sgt. Pepper's Lonely Hearts Club Band* was released in June, critics agreed that the Beatles had made a masterpiece. Twenty years later, *Rolling Stone* magazine called it the best album recorded during the previous two decades.

In their costumes for the *Sgt. Pepper's Lonely Hearts Club Band* record cover

Members of San Francisco's hippie culture in 1967

Sgt. Pepper, however, also caused some trouble for the band. Some people insisted that one of the songs, "Lucy in the Sky With Diamonds," was about the drug LSD, since those letters appeared in the title. John said the idea for the song came from a picture his son Julian had drawn and was not about drugs.

Still, the band had used marijuana and other illegal drugs often since 1964. The Beatles had become a part of the movement that had swept across the United States and Great Britain during the mid-1960s. Many young people, who came to be known as **hippies** or flower children, rejected conventional society and promoted the power of love. Often they used drugs as a way to change their awareness and to heighten their emotions and feelings.

Nevertheless, the Beatles also saw the destructive power of drugs. In August 1967, their manager, Brian Epstein, died from a drug overdose that could have been either intentional or accidental. Epstein had shaped the Beatles' career and helped make them rich. He was also a friend. When Epstein died, George Harrison said, it was "the end of a chapter."

MOVING ON, COMING APART

After Epstein's death, the Beatles began a new project. The group made a movie for British television called *Magical Mystery Tour*. The film was based on Paul's idea about a bus trip through England that seems like a fairy tale. The band also recorded an album with the same name. John said he liked that record because it was "weird." The film, however, was too weird for some people, and it was one of the group's less successful projects.

In 1968, the Beatles went to India to relax and learn how to **meditate**. Meditation consists of sitting quietly and trying to clear the mind of all thoughts. Some people also repeat a word or sound, such as "om," as they meditate. Meditation is practiced in many Eastern religions. As with Indian music, George took the lead in exploring meditation, but the rest of the band also tried it. After returning to England, the Beatles started working on a new album. By now, the group had launched its own company called Apple Corps. The Beatles planned to make films, record other musicians, and sell clothes. Their musical success gave them the power and money to try this new business, something no band before had ever done. The band was also now managing itself, and the members soon learned they were much better musicians than businessmen. Apple's future problems led to disagreements within the band.

Another issue began to create cracks in the band's relationship: the influence of John's new girlfriend, Yoko Ono. John had met this Japanese artist in 1966. In 1968, he and Yoko became a couple. Yoko started coming to the band's recording sessions—something George, Paul, and Ringo did not like. She made suggestions about the music and disrupted the band's usual way of working together. John and Yoko also worked on their own records.

The album the Beatles recorded during the summer of 1968 was called simply *The Beatles*, though everyone soon called it "the White Album,"

Yellow Submarine

Late in 1966, the Beatles approved the idea of an animated movie using characters based on the band. Released in 1968, the movie was called *Yellow Submarine*, the name of a song Paul had written for *Revolver*. The movie featured Beatles songs from several different albums, and the band also recorded several new songs for the film. The Beatles were not actively involved in making *Yellow Submarine*, though they are featured as cartoon characters in the film (above), dressed as they appeared on the *Sgt. Pepper* album cover. Professional actors provided their voices. The real Beatles do make one brief appearance at the end of the movie. One critic called *Yellow Submarine* "a masterpiece" that "opened up new and undreamed horizons for animation."

The Beatles traveled to India in 1968 to learn more about Eastern religions.

John Lennon with Yoko Ono in 1971

because of its plain white cover. The album had two records and thirty songs. Some were not up to the usual Beatle standards, but the album still reached number one on the record charts.

At times during the recording of the White Album, the band members did not see one another. Each musician taped his musical parts on his own. Paul later said the album "wasn't a pleasant one to make." At one point during the recordings, Ringo briefly left the group. He later said he felt left out of the band and did not think he was playing well. The newspapers did not learn about his departure, and within two weeks he was back in the band. Still, the future of the Beatles was becoming more uncertain.

THE END OF THE BEATLES

The grumbling between the Beatles grew worse after the White Album. By now, John was more interested in Yoko and their relationship than playing with the Beatles. In a 1980 interview, he said making music with his old band mates had become a job, nothing more. Paul was trying to keep the group busy, suggesting the Beatles play live or film a concert for television. By now, the other band members sometimes felt Paul was trying too hard to be the "boss" of the Beatles, and this added to the tension.

Early in 1969, the band began rehearsing for a TV special, and things did not start well. With a film crew recording as they rehearsed, Paul and George argued over how George should play a certain song. George also sensed that Yoko was trying to convince John to quit the band. At one point George left the studio and was ready to leave the band for good. "I think the first couple of days were OK," he later said. "But it was soon quite apparent that it was just the same as it had been when we were last in the studio, and it was going to be painful again."

When George came back, he and the others decided to make an album with songs planned for their TV special. This record, first called *Get Back* and then *Let It Be*, was not released until 1970 (the band never made the TV concert). While working on this record, the Beatles played a few songs live from the roof of the Apple Corps building.

An impromptu show on the roof of the Apple Corps building in 1969 proved to be the Beatles' last public performance.

Paul and Linda
McCartney in 1974

John Lennon and Yoko
Ono at a 1969 bed-in in
Amsterdam

Although not a real concert, it was their last live performance in public. The songs were taped and later appeared in the movie *Let It Be*.

When spring came, the Beatles were in the news, but not for their music. In March, Paul married Linda Eastman, and John married Yoko (he had earlier divorced Cynthia). The Lennons then held **bed-ins** for peace. The couple stayed in bed while the media interviewed and filmed them. "In effect," John explained in 1980, "we were doing a commercial for peace." John and Yoko, like many young people of the era, opposed the Vietnam War and other forms of violence.

Later in the year, the band returned to the studio. None of the band members had particularly liked the recordings for *Let It Be*, which they had yet to release, and they wanted to record something better. The result was *Abbey Road*, named for the studio where the Beatles had recorded most of their hits. Once again, the group had a number-one album on the record charts. It also released two number-one songs in 1969, "Get Back" and "Something." With "Get Back," the Beatles turned away from musical experimentation. The band recorded the hard-driving rock 'n' roll song live in the studio. Paul called it "a song to rollercoast by."

BREAKING UP

Despite their continued success, the Beatles were growing farther apart. In the fall of 1969, John and Yoko formed their own band—the Plastic Ono Band. George played guitar with another group, and Ringo released a solo album. The band also argued more about business issues. Paul wanted John Eastman, his new brother-in-law, to handle the group's finances, while the other three wanted accountant Allen Klein. Eventually, John, George, and Ringo signed a contract with Klein, but Paul refused.

To John, the Beatles broke up when he formed his new band. The others also knew then that their group was over, but no one talked about it. Ringo said, "Allen Klein had this thing: 'Split up, boys, if you want to—but don't tell anybody.' . . . It was a relief once we finally said we would split up."

That decision came early in 1970. Paul had recorded a solo record, and the other Beatles, backed by Klein, wanted him to delay its release. The Beatles were finally getting ready to release *Let It Be*. Paul was upset with the way that record sounded, as Klein had brought in a new producer to make changes. On April 10, Paul said publicly that the group had split up, confirming what the band had known for several months.

Paul Is Dead?

Shortly after the release of *Abbey Road*, a U.S. disc jockey started the rumor that Paul was dead and the Beatles were using someone who looked like Paul in his place. According to the DJ, many Beatles' songs and album covers offered "clues" about the death, which supposedly occurred in 1966. John's reaction to the rumor: "Paul McCartney couldn't die without the world knowing it. The same as he couldn't get married without the world knowing it. It's impossible—he can't go on holiday without the world knowing it. It's just insanity—but it's a great plug for *Abbey Road*."

ALWAYS THE BEATLES

Although Beatles fans were stunned, the band members welcomed the split. They had spent most of their teenage and young adult years together. Now they were ready to move on. Still, the Beatles had good memories

Paul and Linda McCartney shown with McCartney's group, Wings, in 1972

Paying tribute at Strawberry Fields, a memorial to John Lennon in New York City's Central Park

of their accomplishments. "It was a really great rock 'n' roll band," said Ringo, "and we made a lot of good music which is still here today."

All the Beatles remained active in music after the breakup. Paul had the most popular success, with his band, Wings, and he later wrote classical music. Ringo also had several hit songs and continued to act in films. He also appeared on a children's TV show and toured with all-star bands that played some Beatles songs. George released solo albums and also became a successful movie producer. He died of cancer in 2001. John's solo career ended with his death in 1980, at a time when he seemed ready to produce some of his most creative music since the end of the Beatles.

The Beatles continue to fascinate fans. Through the years, Capitol Records has released several greatest-hits collections and live albums. Other companies have released tapes from the band's early days. During the 1970s, a stage show called *Beatlemania* offered a musical history of the group with musicians dressed to look like the Fab Four at different stages in their careers. In 2000, Capitol released the CD *1*, a collection of all the group's number-one hits in the United States and Great Britain. The Beatles' films are still shown on TV, and some rock bands still try to copy the Beatles sound.

Before the Beatles, only Elvis Presley had stirred so much excitement in the rock music world. Presley, however, rarely wrote his own songs and barely played guitar. The Beatles truly created their own style of rock 'n' roll. They made rock music a part of life for baby boomers. George said, "I'd like to think that the old Beatles fans have grown up . . . and they're all more responsible, but they still have a space in their hearts for us." Around the world, people of all ages still have space in their hearts for the Beatles, and the band has a special place in the history of rock 'n' roll.

A record owner holding copies of *Sgt. Pepper's Lonely Hearts Club Band* in 1987, twenty years after its release

A Beatles Discography

The following is a list of the major Beatles albums released in Great Britain (GB) and the United States (US) between 1963 and 1970.

1963
Please Please Me (GB)
With the Beatles (GB)

1964
Introducing the Beatles (US)
Meet the Beatles (US)
The Beatles' Second Album (US)
A Hard Day's Night (both)
Something New (US)
Beatles for Sale (GB)
Beatles '65 (US)

1965
Beatles IV (US)
Help! (both)
Rubber Soul (both)

1966
Revolver (both)
Yesterday . . . and Today (US)

1967
Sgt. Pepper's Lonely Hearts Club Band (both)
Magical Mystery Tour (US)

1968
The Beatles (the White Album—both)

1969
Yellow Submarine (both)
Abbey Road (both)

1970
Hey Jude (US)
Let It Be (both)

TIMELINE

1940   Richard Starkey (Ringo Starr) is born on July 7; John Lennon is born on October 9

1942   Paul McCartney is born on June 18

1943   George Harrison is born on February 25

1957   John forms the Quarry Men, and Paul later joins the group

1958   George joins the Quarry Men

1960   The Quarry Men become the Beatles; the group plays in Hamburg, Germany

1962   Brian Epstein becomes the Beatles' manager; Ringo becomes the group's drummer; the band records its first single

1963   "Please Please Me" is the Beatles first number-one hit in Great Britain; Beatlemania begins

1964   Beatlemania spreads to America as the group makes its historic appearance on *The Ed Sullivan Show*

1965   Movie *Help!* is released; George discovers Indian music; album *Rubber Soul* indicates growth in the Beatles' talents

1966   Beatles give last live concert; release *Revolver*

1967   Group releases *Sgt. Pepper*; Brian Epstein dies

1968   *The Beatles* album and the movie *Yellow Submarine* are released

1969   Beatles record songs that will appear on *Let It Be*; also record film of their last public performance, on roof of Apple Corps building; band releases album *Abbey Road*

1970   *Let It Be* is released; "The Long and Winding Road" is the group's last number-one hit; Paul records a solo album and says publicly that the Beatles will not work together again

1980   John Lennon is shot and killed outside his home in New York City on December 8

2001   George Harrison dies of cancer in Los Angeles on November 29

GLOSSARY

acoustic: a type of instrument that does not use electronics

baby boom: an era in the United States, roughly between 1946 and 1964, in which large number of babies were born, compared to the years of the Great Depression and World War II

Beatlemania: a term created by journalists to describe the huge early popularity of the Beatles

bed-ins: events staged by John Lennon and Yoko Ono in hotel bedrooms to promote peace

blues: a musical style developed primarily by African-Americans, often with lyrics describing personal loss or suffering and originally played on acoustic instruments

British Invasion: a wave of British groups that became popular after the success of the Beatles

chords: combinations of three or more musical notes played at the same time

flip side: the second or "b" side of a single, usually containing a less popular song

gospel: church music developed primarily by African-Americans with simple melodies and elements of the blues

harmonium: a type of organ that uses reeds

hippies: members of a youth movement in the 1960s and 1970s; they believed in love and peace, and they rejected materialism

meditate: to relax and clear the mind of thoughts; meditation is part of some religions as well as a relaxation technique

overdubbing: recording instruments or voices onto a tape that already has music on it, combining the sounds

producer: a person who controls a recording session for a musical act, making suggestions on what instruments are used or how a song should be played

record chart: a list of the most popular records or CDs

reeds: small pieces of wood, cane, or metal that vibrate to make sounds in some musical instruments

rhythm and blues: African-American music that combines the blues with a strong beat

sitar: a musical instrument from India

skiffle: a form of folk music popular in Great Britain during the 1950s that featured simple instruments, such as acoustic guitars and washboards

variety show: a television program featuring musical acts, comedians, and other entertainers

TO FIND OUT MORE

BOOKS

The Beatles. *The Beatles Anthology.* San Francisco: Chronicle Books, 2000.

The Beatles Complete Chord Songbook. Milwaukee: Hal Leonard, 1999.

Conord, Bruce W. *John Lennon*. New York: Chelsea House, 1994.

Holland, Gini. *The 1960s*. San Diego: Lucent Books, 1999.

Roberts, Jeremy. *The Beatles*. Minneapolis: Lerner Publications, 2001.

Woog, Adam. *The Beatles*. San Diego: Lucent Books, 1998.

INTERNET SITES

The Beatles 1
www.thebeatles.com
A multimedia site with audio, video, and text for each of the twenty-seven songs on *The Beatles 1* greatest-hits collection.

Beatles Internet Resource Guide
www.beatlelinks.net
A site with links to many of the hundreds of websites devoted to the Beatles, including fan clubs and pages with the band's lyrics.

George Harrison—All Things Must Pass
www.allthingsmustpass.com
The official site for George Harrison as a solo artist.

Instant Karma! The John and Yoko Magazine
www.instantkarma.com
Created by a fan; features articles on John Lennon and Yoko Ono, as well as John's two children, Julian and Sean.

Paul McCartney
www.mplcommunications.com/mccartney/ index.htm
The official site for Paul McCartney; has a detailed biography and news on his career.

Ringo Tour.com
www.ringotour.com/2001/index.htm
A site dedicated to Ringo Starr's annual tour with an all-star band, which plays Beatles music and songs by the other musicians.

INDEX

INDEX *(continued)*

About the Author

As an editor at *Weekly Reader* for six years, **Michael Burgan** created educational material for an interactive online service and wrote on current events. Now a freelance author, Michael has written more than 30 books, primarily for children and young adults. These include biographies of Secretary of State Madeleine Albright, Presidents John Adams and John F. Kennedy, and astronaut John Glenn. His other historical writings include two volumes in the series *American Immigration* and the four-volume set *Cold War.* Michael has a BA in history from the University of Connecticut and resides in that state.